Bank Tellers
Community Workers

by Cynthia Klingel and Robert B. Noyed

Content Adviser: Brian Jessen, Vice President,
Residential Lending, Harris Bank, Chicago

Reading Adviser: Dr. Linda D. Labbo,
College of Education, Department of Reading Education,
The University of Georgia

COMPASS POINT BOOKS

Minneapolis, Minnesota

Compass Point Books
3722 West 50th Street, #115
Minneapolis, MN 55410

Visit Compass Point Books on the Internet at *www.compasspointbooks.com* or e-mail your request to *custserv@compasspointbooks.com*

Editors: E. Russell Primm, Emily J. Dolbear, and Pam Rosenberg
Photo Researcher: Svetlana Zhurkina
Photo Selector: Linda S. Koutris
Designer: Bradfordesign, Inc.

Library of Congress Cataloging-in-Publication Data

Klingel, Cynthia Fitterer.
    Bank tellers / by Cynthia Klingel and Robert B. Noyed; content adviser, Brian Jessen; reading adviser, Linda D. Labbo.
        p. cm. — (Community workers)
    Summary: Introduces the job of bank teller, including the duties, skills, physical requirements, and contribution to the community.
    Includes bibliographical references and index.
    ISBN 0-7565-0307-8
        1. Bank tellers—Juvenile literature. [1. Bank tellers. 2. Occupations.] I. Noyed, Robert B. II. Title. III. Series.
    HG1615.7.T4 K58 2003
    332.1'2—dc21   2002003036

Table of Contents

What Do Bank Tellers Do?

Bank tellers help people **deposit** and **withdraw** money from the bank. Bank tellers also cash **checks** for people. Some bank tellers buy and sell money from other countries. Bank tellers may also accept **mortgage** and other loan payments.

◀ Bank tellers handle both checks and cash.

A customer hands cash to the teller to make a loan payment. ▶

What Tools and Equipment Do They Use?

A bank teller uses a cash drawer. When customers withdraw money, it is taken from the drawer. When they deposit money, it is added to the drawer. Bank tellers use computers to keep track of the money taken in and paid out. They also use calculators to add and subtract.

Bank tellers remove their cash drawers from the bank vault every day and place them in their work stations.

A bank teller uses a calculator to add numbers.

How Do Bank Tellers Help?

Bank tellers help the community by helping people manage their money. Maybe your dad needs to cash his paycheck. The bank teller can cash the check for him. Maybe your mom needs to make the monthly mortgage payment on your house. The bank teller can accept that payment.

◀ A bank customer cashes a check.

The bank teller ▶ processes a loan payment.

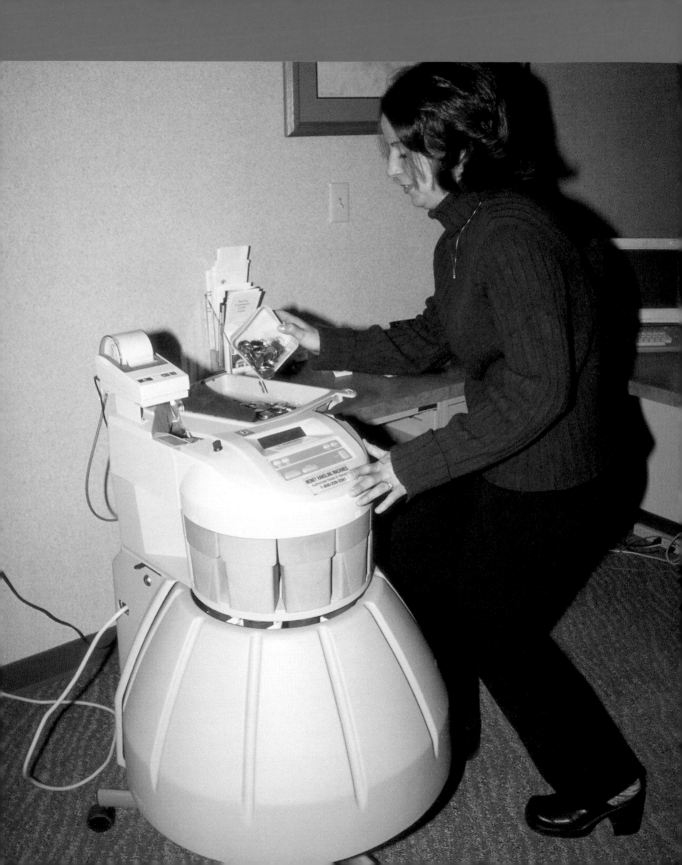

Have you been saving money in your piggy bank for something special? Maybe you would like to know how much money you have. The bank teller can count your coins with a special machine and give you paper money in exchange. Now you can go shopping or decide to keep saving your money!

A special machine counts coins.

This child makes a deposit to her savings account.

Where Do Bank Tellers Work?

Bank tellers work in banks. Most work at teller windows in the bank. The teller windows are usually in the lobby of the bank. Some bank tellers work at drive-up teller windows. Bank customers do their banking from their cars. Some tellers work in walk-up windows. Customers can bank from the sidewalk!

◀ This teller works in the drive-up area.

A teller supervisor ▶ opens the cash vault each morning.

With Whom Do Bank Tellers Work?

Bank tellers work with head tellers or teller **supervisors**. They also work with personal bankers and bank officers. Personal bankers open bank accounts for customers. Bank officers lend money to people and businesses. Bank tellers also work with security guards. These guards keep employees and customers safe.

◀ A teller supervisor helps a teller with a computer question.

Tellers chat with a lobby security guard. ▶

What Do Bank Tellers Wear?

Bank tellers must always be well groomed, neat, and clean. Male tellers usually wear dress pants and dress shirts with ties. They sometimes wear sport coats. Female tellers usually wear skirts or slacks and shirts. Sometimes they wear business suits.

◄ Male bank tellers wear dress pants and shirts.

Female bank tellers often wear suits. ►

What Training Does It Take?

Bank tellers must have a high school diploma. They must be good in mathematics. They must also know how to use computers and calculators. They might take special classes at the bank or at a school. These classes may help them learn more about the work done at a bank.

◄ Learning good math skills is important for future bank tellers.

Knowing how ► to use a computer is also important.

What Skills Do Bank Tellers Need?

Bank tellers must be accurate in their work. Bank tellers also have to deal with people. They must have a pleasant personality and good manners. Bank tellers work with large amounts of money. The bank's owners and customers trust the bank tellers with their money. Honesty is the most important quality of all.

◀ A pleasant manner and nice smile are good assets for bank tellers.

Bank tellers must be accurate in their work. ▶

What Problems Do They Face?

Bank tellers have to work quickly. They try to make no mistakes. At the end of each day, tellers must find any mistakes. Sometimes people try to steal money from banks. Knowing that a robbery is possible may be stressful for bank tellers.

◀ Bank tellers work hard to keep from making mistakes in giving back cash.

Security cameras help keep the bank safe. ▶

Would You Like to Be a Bank Teller?

Do you like math? Do you like working with money? Do you like helping people? Do you take pride in being honest? Maybe you would like to be a bank teller someday. You can prepare now. Work hard in math class at school. Learn how to use a computer. Go to the bank with your savings and open a bank account.

◀ Two boys pretend to be bank tellers!

A girl practices ▶ her computer skills.

A Bank Teller's Tools and Clothes

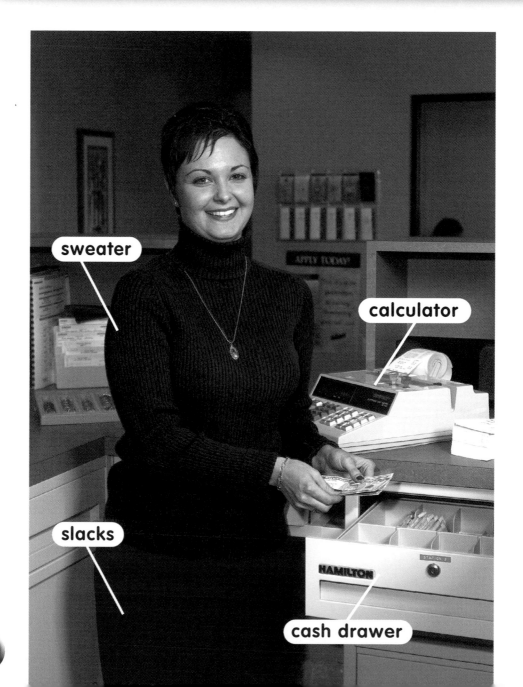

sweater

calculator

slacks

cash drawer

HAMILTON

At the Bank

calculator

computer

printer

desk

cash drawer

office chair

A Bank Teller's Day

Morning
- The bank teller arrives at the bank. He picks up his cash drawer from the vault.
- He goes to the teller window where he will be working and organizes his supplies.
- He greets his first customer of the day. He helps her deposit a check in her savings account.
- Another customer wants to open a checking account. The bank teller sends him to see a bank officer.

Noon
- The bank teller locks up his cash drawer and goes to lunch.
- At lunch he talks with other bank employees about taking some training classes. He would like to learn more about banking. He hopes to become a bank officer someday.

Afternoon
- A customer wants to withdraw $3,000 from her account. The teller carefully checks her identification and bank balance. He wants to be sure he is giving the money to the right person.
- His supervisor tells him to close his window. He takes his cash drawer and carefully checks all his work for the day.
- After he checks his work, he goes home for the day.

Evening
- The bank teller has dinner with his family.
- He goes to bed early. He must be at work by 6:45 A.M. to open the drive-up window at 7:00 A.M.

Glossary

checks—printed pieces of paper that order a bank to pay a certain amount of money to a certain person or business

counterfeit—fake

deposit—to put in

mortgage—a loan from a bank to buy a house or a piece of land

supervisors—people who direct and watch over the work of others

withdraw—to take out

Did You Know?

- The word *bank* comes from the Italian word *banco,* which means "bench." Italy was an important center of banking in the Middle Ages. Bankers sat on benches in the public square and exchanged money for their customers.

- The Bank of North America was the first bank in the United States. It was founded in 1782.

- During the U.S. Civil War (1861–1865), between one-third and one-half of the paper money in circulation was **counterfeit** money.

- The U.S. Secret Service was created to stop counterfeiters.

Want to Know More?

At the Library

Bagley, Katie, Lois J. Schuldt, and Shannon Duffy. *Bank Tellers*. Mankato, Minn.: Capstone Press, 2001.

Hall, Margaret. *Banks*. Chicago: Heinemann Library, 2000.

Sirimarco, Elizabeth. *At the Bank*. Eden Prairie, Minn.: The Child's World, 1999.

On the Web

KidsBank.com

http://www.kidsbank.com/index.asp

To learn more about banking

The United States Mint

http://www.usmint.gov/

To see new and special coins

Through the Mail

American Bankers Association

1120 Connecticut Avenue, N.W.

Washington, DC 20036

800/338-0626

To get more information about banking

On the Road

The United States Mint

151 North Independence Mall East

Philadelphia, PA 19106-1886

215/408-0114

To tour the nation's oldest mint

Index

About the Authors

Cynthia Klingel has worked as a high school English teacher and an elementary school teacher. She is currently the curriculum director for a Minnesota school district. Cynthia Klingel lives with her family in Mankato, Minnesota.

Robert B. Noyed started his career as a newspaper reporter. Since then, he has worked in school communications and public relations at the state and national level. Robert B. Noyed lives with his family in Brooklyn Center, Minnesota.